To Cecilia & Tom in
memory of Ryan.
Frances & J.D.

THE GREATEST
OF THESE
IS
LOVE

GOD'S HOLY WORDS

MINGLED WITH ROSES
By Hazel Hoffman

VERSES AND AFFECTIONATE
SENTIMENTS
By Audrey McDaniel

A gift of favorite passages.
They can answer in perfect
sequence our every need.
HE LEFT US THE WORD . . .
We have only to inquire of
these loving "Scriptures".

" . . . . May LOVE open the book,
and FAITH turn its pages . . . . "

"He left us the Word . . . . ."

TEACH ME TO PRAY:
Matthew 6: 9 through 13

Our Father which art in heaven,
Hallowed be thy name.
Thy kingdom come.
Thy will be done in earth,
    as it is in heaven.
Give us this day our daily bread.
And forgive us our debts, as we
    forgive our debtors.
And lead us not into temptation,
    but deliver us from evil:
For thine is the kingdom, and the
    power, and the glory, for ever.
                                Amen.

THY WILL BE DONE:

Eloquent words like diamonds and pearls
imprinted on the hearts of men through
this life and eternity as Jesus spake teach-
ing them to pray . . . .

"He left us the Word . . . . ."

The most unselfish prayer of all.

FATHER, THE HOUR IS COME:

John 17:   1, 4, 6, 9

I have glorified thee on the earth: I have finished the work which thou gavest me to do.

I have manifested thy name unto the men which thou gavest me out of the world: thine they were, and thou gavest them me; and they have kept thy word.

I pray for them: I pray not for the world, but for them which thou hast given me; for they are thine.

I AM PRAYING FOR THEM:

Here Jesus is sponsoring us before God in His final hour; not praying for His own concern, but beseeching God to have faith in us. NOTHING will ever reach the heights of devotion found in "I AM PRAYING FOR THEM"

5

LORD make me an instrument of Thy peace;
Where there is hatred, let me sow love;
Where there is doubt, faith;
Where there is despair, hope;
Where there is darkness, light;
and where there is sadness, joy.

O DIVINE MASTER, grant that I may not so much seek to be consoled, as to console; to be understood, as to understand; to be loved, as to love; for it is in giving that we receive, it is in pardoning that we are pardoned, and it is in dying that we are born to eternal life.

ST. FRANCIS

THE TEN COMMANDMENTS
Deuteronomy 5

Thou shalt have none other gods before me.
Thou shalt not make thee any graven image.
Thou shalt not take the name of the Lord thy
    God in vain.
Keep the sabbath day to sanctify it.
Honour thy father and thy mother.
Thou shalt not kill.
Thou shalt not commit adultery.
Thou shalt not steal.
Thou shalt not bear false witness against
    thy neighbour.
Thou shalt not covet.

IF YE KEEP MY COMMANDMENTS:

Ye shall abide in my love.

John 15: 10

7

"He left us the Word . . . ."

THE BEATITUDES:
Matthew 5:   2 through 12

And he opened his mouth, and taught
    them, saying,
Blessed are the poor in spirit: for theirs
    is the kingdom of heaven.
Blessed are they that mourn: for they
    shall be comforted.
Blessed are the meek: for they shall
    inherit the earth.
Blessed are they which do hunger and
    thirst after righteousness: for
    they shall be filled.
Blessed are the merciful: for they
    shall obtain mercy.
Blessed are the pure in heart: for they
    shall see God.
Blessed are the peacemakers: for they
    shall be called the children of God.
Blessed are they which are persecuted
    for righteousness' sake: for theirs
    is the kingdom of heaven.
Blessed are ye, when men shall revile
    you, and persecute you, and shall
    say all manner of evil against
    you falsely, for my sake.
Rejoice, and be exceeding glad: for
    great is your reward in heaven:
    for so persecuted they the
    prophets which were before you.

"He left us the Word . . . ."

Psalms 23

The Lord is my shepherd; I shall
    not want.
He maketh me to lie down in green
    pastures:
He leadeth me beside the still waters.
He restoreth my soul:
He leadeth me in the paths of
    righteousness for
    his name's sake.

Yea, though I walk through the
    valley of the shadow of death,
I will fear no evil:
For thou art with me;
Thy rod and thy staff
They comfort me.

Thou preparest a table before me
    in the presence of mine enemies:
Thou anointest my head with oil;
My cup runneth over.
Surely goodness and mercy shall
    follow me all the days
    of my life:
And I will dwell in the house
    of the Lord for ever.

"He left us the Word . . . . ."

STEPPING STONES TO GOD:
Romans 12:   9, 10, 11, 12, 14, 15, 18, 21

Let love be without dissimulation.
Abhor that which is evil; cleave
to that which is good.

Be kindly affectioned one to another.

Not slothful in business; fervent
in spirit; serving the Lord;

Rejoicing in hope; patient in tribulation;
continuing instant in prayer;

Bless them which persecute you:
bless, and curse not.

Rejoice with them that do rejoice,
and weep with them that weep.

If it be possible, as much as lieth in you,
live peaceably with all men.

Be not overcome of evil, but
overcome evil with good.

"He left us the Word . . . ."

WHEN THE HEART IS TROUBLED:
Romans 8:   35 through 39

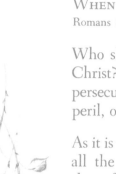

Who shall separate us from the love of Christ? shall tribulation, or distress, or persecution, or famine, or nakedness, or peril, or sword?

As it is written, For thy sake we are killed all the day long; we are accounted as sheep for the slaughter.

Nay, in all these things we are more than conquerors through him that loved us.

For I am persuaded, that neither death, nor life, nor angels, nor principalities, nor powers, nor things present, nor things to come,

Nor height, nor depth, nor any other creature, shall be able to separate us from the love of God, which is in Christ Jesus our Lord.

THINK ON THESE THINGS:

Nothing shall separate us --

"He left us the Word . . . . ."

FAITH:
Matthew 17: 20

And Jesus said unto them, Because of your unbelief: for verily I say unto you, If ye have faith as a grain of mustard seed, ye shall say unto this mountain, Remove hence to yonder place; and it shall remove; and nothing shall be impossible unto you.

Mark 9: 23

Jesus said unto him, If thou canst believe, all things are possible to him that believeth.

MY FAITH LOOKS UP TO THEE:

May the light of your faith so shine that it will illuminate the heart of another.

"He left us the Word . . . . ."

To help us find hope:
Romans 8: 24, 25, 28

For we are saved by hope: but hope that is seen is not hope: for what a man seeth, why doth he yet hope for?

But if we hope for that we see not, then do we with patience wait for it.

And we know that all things work together for good to them that love God, to them who are the called according to his purpose.

I AM GRATEFUL FOR
THESE LOVING PROMISES TO LEAN ON:

In Him nothing is hopeless . . . .
And He is always near.
Beams of light from the halo
    of His loving head
Shall illuminate our path to
    HOPE.

"He left us the Word . . . ."

LOVE:
I Corinthians 13: 1, 2, 3, 13

Though I speak with the tongues of men and of angels, and have not love, I am become as sounding brass, or a tinkling cymbal.

And though I have the gift of prophecy, and understand all mysteries, and all knowledge; and though I have all faith, so that I could remove mountains, and have not love, I am nothing.

And though I bestow all my goods to feed the poor, and though I give my body to be burned, and have not love, it profiteth me nothing.

And now abideth faith, hope, love, these three; but the greatest of these is love.

WHAT IS BEYOND LOVE . . . . ?
THE ANSWER IS NOTHING

Love bears all things, believes all things, hopes all things, endures all things, Love never ends.

"He left us the Word . . . . . "

HIS PROMISE TO ANSWER OUR NEEDS:
Mark 11:   22 through 24

And Jesus answering saith unto them, Have faith in God.

For verily I say unto you, That whosoever shall say unto this mountain, Be thou removed, and be thou cast into the sea; and shall not doubt in his heart, but shall believe that those things which he saith shall come to pass; he shall have whatsoever he saith.

Therefore I say unto you, What things soever ye desire, when ye pray, believe that ye receive them, and ye shall have them.

AND NOT DOUBT IN OUR HEARTS:

God knows our needs before we make our supplications, and when we receive His answers they are more wonderful than we would have known to ask for.

15

"He left us the Word . . . . "

Matthew 7: 7, 8

Ask, and it shall be given you; seek, and ye shall find; knock, and it shall be opened unto you:

For every one that asketh receiveth; and he that seeketh findeth; and to him that knocketh it shall be opened.

HE HEARETH THEE:

We have only to make a passionate utterance in faith -- Believing -- and He is only a prayer away.

"He left us the Word . . . ."

To HELP US FIND CONFIDENCE:
John 14: 14, 18, 27

If ye shall ask any thing in my name, I will do it.

I will not leave you comfortless: I will come to you.

Peace I leave with you, my peace I give unto you: not as the world giveth, give I unto you. Let not your heart be troubled, neither let it be afraid.

I John 5: 14

And this is the confidence that we have in him, that if we ask any thing according to his will, he heareth us:

HE GAVE US THESE PROMISES:

Have faith in the Master.

"He left us the Word . . . . ."

To overcome life's anxieties:
Luke 12: 27, 28, 29, 31

Consider the lilies how they grow: they toil not, they spin not; and yet I say unto you, that Solomon in all his glory was not arrayed like one of these.

If then God so clothe the grass which is today in the field, and tomorrow is cast into the oven; how much more will he clothe you, O ye of little faith?

And seek not ye what ye shall eat, or what ye shall drink, neither be ye of doubtful mind.

But rather seek ye the kingdom of God; and all these things shall be added unto you.

For where your treasure is, there will your heart be also.
Luke 12: 34

Put your heart at rest . . . . He has blessings unending waiting for us, if we live to please him.

"He left us the Word . . . . ."

MORE ABOUT LOVE:
John 3: 16

For God so loved the world, that he gave his only begotten Son, that whosoever believeth in him should not perish, but have everlasting life.

I John 4: 19
We love him, because he first loved us.

I John 4: 8
He that loveth not knoweth not God; for God is love.

I John 4: 11
Beloved, if God so loved us, we ought also to love one another.

IT HAS TAKEN AUTHORS HUNDREDS OF WORDS TO SAY WHAT JESUS SUMMED UP IN THREE WORDS -- "GOD IS LOVE".

Make love your aim.

"He left us the Word . . . ."

FRIENDS:
John 15: 12 through 14

This is my commandment, That ye love one another, as I have loved you.

Greater love hath no man than this, that a man lay down his life for his friends.

Ye are my friends, if ye do whatsoever I command you.

HE CHOSE US AS HIS FRIENDS:

And as our reward we are sheltered and shall abide in His love forever.

"He left us the Word . . . . ."

FOR OTHERS:
Luke 4: 18

The Spirit of the Lord is upon me, because he hath anointed me to preach the
gospel to the poor; he hath sent me to
heal the brokenhearted, to preach deliv-
erance to the captives, and recovering of
sight to the blind, to set at liberty them
that are bruised.

FULFILLING LOVE:

Once in a while someone lives a beauti-
ful and totally unselfish life -- "Just for
Others".

As if their only prayers were "Lord, let
me live for others. Let me knock on every
door and mend every troubled heart".

To them every individual in their life,
regardless of relationship or compati-
bility, is a friend from God. They feel,
if they fail to love and serve them, they
hurt the GIVER first.

Our Saviour gave HIS ALL upon a rugged
cross for OTHERS.

21

"He left us the Word . . . ."

SERVING . . . . HIS WAY:
Matthew 6: 3, 6

But when thou doest alms, let not thy left hand know what thy right hand doeth:

But thou, when thou prayest, enter into thy closet, and when thou hast shut thy door, pray to thy Father which is in secret; and thy Father which seeth in secret shall reward thee openly.

MAY WE GIVE LOVE AND SHOW MERCY AND SERVE HUMBLY TO PLEASE GOD.

In the secret hours of our lives may we be about our Father's work.

"He left us the Word . . . . ."

DIVORCE:
Matthew 19: 6 through 8

What therefore God hath joined together, let not man put asunder.

They say unto him, Why did Moses then
command to give a writing of divorce-
ment, and to put her away?

He saith unto them, Moses because of
the hardness of your hearts suffered you
to put away your wives; but from the be-
ginning it was not so.

I Corinthians 7: 16, 17

For what knowest thou, O wife, whether
thou shalt save thy husband? or how
knowest thou, O man, whether thou
shalt save thy wife?

And so ordain I in all churches.

WE HAVE A MISSION TO DO:

We have the mission of living together
in our separate ways, as we love.

"He left us the Word . . . ."

SIN:
Romans 6: 12, 14, 17, 22, 23

Let not sin therefore reign in your mortal body, that ye should obey it in the lusts thereof.

For sin shall not have dominion over you: for ye are not under the law, but under grace.

God be thanked, that ye were the servants of sin, but ye have obeyed from the heart that form of doctrine which was delivered you.

Now being made free from sin, and become servants to God, ye have your fruit unto holiness, and the end everlasting life.

For the wages of sin is death; but the gift of God is eternal life through Jesus Christ our Lord.

O PRECIOUS GIFT:

Put your heart at rest.

"He left us the Word . . . . ."

FORGIVENESS:
Mark 11:   25, 26

And when ye stand praying, forgive, if ye
have ought against any: that your Father
also which is in heaven may forgive you
your trespasses.

But if ye do not forgive, neither will your
Father which is in heaven forgive your
trespasses.

THE GREATEST OF ALL:

Father, forgive them; for they know not
what they do.

Luke 23:   34

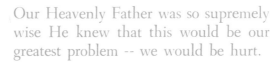

"He left us the Word . . . ."

COMPASSION:
Proverbs 15: 1

A soft answer turneth away wrath: but grievous words stir up anger.

DO GOOD TO THEM THAT HURT YOU:

Our Heavenly Father was so supremely wise He knew that this would be our greatest problem -- we would be hurt.

In His magnanimous intelligence He left us the Word . . . . LOVE THY NEIGHBOUR AS THYSELF. And He stressed it as the Second Greatest Commandment.

Try to believe that unkind hearts are often troubled souls. In their disagreement, they are only crying out to us *not* to leave them -- not loving them -- but to draw closer to them in understanding.

Search for good in the hearts of all.

"He left us the Word . . . ."

FOR THE WEARY:
Matthew 11:   28 through 30

Come unto me, all ye that labour and
are heavy laden, and I will give you rest.

Take my yoke upon you, and learn of
me; for I am meek and lowly in heart:
and ye shall find rest unto your souls.

For my yoke is easy, and my burden is
light.

I Peter 5:   7

Casting all your care upon him; for he
careth for you.

TAKE YOUR BURDENS TO THE LORD
IN PRAYER:

He will undo the heavy burdened, and
let the oppressed go free.

"He left us the Word . . . . . "

SOMETHING TO LOOK FORWARD TO:
John 14: 1 through 3

Let not your heart be troubled: ye believe in God, believe also in me.

In my Father's house are many mansions: if it were not so, I would have told you. I go to prepare a place for you.

And if I go and prepare a place for you, I will come again, and receive you unto myself; that where I am, there ye may be also.

IN MY FATHER'S HOUSE:

Teach me thy way O Lord . . . .

"He left us the Word . . . ."

FOR THE BEREAVED:
John 14: 6

I am the way, the truth, and the life:

THOUGH THEY WERE DEAD, YET SHALL THEY LIVE:

O dry those tears, God has them in "His Arms", the only one we would want to trust them to. They were only loaned to us. We have given these PRECIOUS GEMS back to God. Now they are numbered among the angels.

The things they stand for are from everlasting to everlasting. Only we can pull the shades of gloom to our hearts to shut them out.

From the Cradle to the Cross we would profess to teach them to be brave and to look up to God. Now, with faith in our hearts as they look down on us, may we profess our courage.

They left us an unfinished mission. Now may we pay tribute to them as we re-dedicate our love to God to finish the broken refrain - - the broken sentiment - - they started in our lives.

They will look down on us in loving gratitude.

"He left us the Word . . . . ."

CHURCH ATTENDANCE:

The Steeple beckons Look Up —
HIGH UP — — in Faith to God.

A LOVING INVITATION:

He does not force us to attend Church
. . . He only lovingly invites, as if to say
"Thou shalt build an edifice in My
Name and I invite you to come."

In the quietude of His sacred Sanctuary
our misdoings shall be secretly forgiven
without embarrassment or betrayal.

We can lay our burdens on the seat and
when we leave He gathers these sad-
nesses and heartbreaks from row to row
and removes them hence, casting them
into the sea forever to fulfill the beauti-
ful, "Casting your burdens upon Him
for He careth for you."

What could be more inspiring than to
know HERE He can fill us with the HOLY
SPIRIT until we hear HIM SPEAK?

Let the
words
of
my mouth,
and the
meditations
of
my heart,
be
acceptable
in thy
sight . . .

Psalms 19: 14

Who created a flower to bloom,
Who designed a prayer,
Who dreamed up the joy of love?
-- Only the God we share.

NOW BLOSSOMS GETHSEMANE

Birds' songs bursting everywhere,
Gorgeous flowers perfume the air
Scriptures fulfilled by His PRAYER
And His love still lingers there.
In this place of sweet repose
God gave us a precious ROSE.

MIDST THE ROSES

He will take us in the Garden
We will kneel, and He will pardon
As we pause beside Him praying
We will hear our Master saying:
Give your hearts to Me this day
In the Garden we will stay.

Midst the sunshine and the flowers
Life will seem like Heavenly bowers
And our hearts will turn to singing
And our souls with joy be ringing
As we sigh and dream and pray
On that gorgeous sacred way.

We will put our arms around Him
We will kneel because we've found Him
With our love we will caress Him
With our hearts we will possess Him
And we'll walk there every day
With our Saviour just to pray.

FATHER FORGIVE

Father forgive, they know not
    what they do
That thou didst send Me
To teach the way to You
In sweet compassion
For them I pray
Trust them, believe them,
Keep them this day
Strengthen their faith in
    My love so true
Father forgive them, they
    know not what they do.

Father forgive, they know not
    what they do
That I was pleading
To bring them to You
In tender passion
Again I pray
Guide them, please Father
Love them this day
Inspire their hearts to
    serve Thee anew
Father forgive them, they
    know not what they do.

ON THE WAY TO GOD

They say each day has its
        Cross to bear
That could make one think
There's no joy to share.
But for me the Cross
At the end of my dreams
Is the goal that shapes
        my spiritual schemes.
Its veils of gloom
Have dropped to the ground
And ROSES and LOVE
Have replaced its Crown
And there by that symbol
That sacred retreat
Is my Heavenly Father
For me to meet.

HIS PRESENCE

Father, take my hand in Thine
Let me serve through love Divine
If some heart should lose its way
Let me be the one to pray
Like a candle shed the light
Till Thy Presence is in sight.

I would tell them o'er and o'er
Thou art just outside the door
Their heart's latch is from within
Open wide and let Thee in
In temptation or despair
Thou art always standing there.

Then I'd ask dear Father Mine
Bless their lives with joy sublime
If they serve Thee all the way
Come into their hearts and stay
Fill their souls with sacred love
Till they live with Thee above.

THAT'S WHAT I LOVE
ABOUT GOD

We have never gone to Him
and found Him not there
His love has always been
consistently the same
As strong at the eventide
as it was at the dawning
We will never go to Him
and find Him not there
We will never seek Him
trying to do better
and He not hear
And we will never do better
and not find that He
rewards us.

"He left us the Word . . . ."

THE BENEDICTION:
Numbers 6: 24 through 26

The Lord bless thee, and keep thee:
The Lord make his face shine upon thee,
And be gracious unto thee:
The Lord lift up his countenance upon
    thee,
And give thee peace.

Amen.

AS WE PART ONE FROM THE OTHER:

And the peace of God, which passeth all
understanding, shall keep your hearts
and minds through Christ Jesus.

Phillipians 4: 7

39

" . . . . *And he closed the book,*
and he gave it again to the
minister . . . . "

Luke 4: 20